7 LESSONS TO INTRODUCE YOUR CHILD TO BIBLICAL SEXUALITY

LUKE GILKERSON

INTOXICATEDONLIFE.COM

STOP! Before You Get Started...

Luke and Trisha Gilkerson

WATCH THESE 3 *FREE* VIDEOS

Thank you for purchasing our book! Take a moment to check out 3 free videos we've put together on talking to kids about sex. We'll teach you...

- The 2 essential Biblical truths about sex you must pass on to your kids
- 3 parenting style you want to be sure to avoid
- Why it's important to begin talking about sex sooner than you think

IntoxicatedOnLife.com/TalkVideos

Contents

Changes: 7 Biblical Lessons to Make Sense of Puberty
is the second in a series of devotional books for families focusing on sex education.

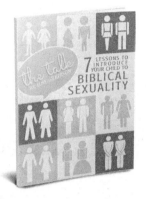

The Talk: 7 Lessons to Introduce Your Child to Biblical Sexuality
This book is for kids ages 6-10 and introduces basic concepts, such as the differences between male and female anatomy, how babies are conceived and grow in the womb, and the importance of saving sex until marriage.

Changes: 7 Biblical Lessons to Make Sense of Puberty – This book is geared towards kids ages 8-12 and introduces children to the physical and emotional changes that puberty brings. Go to IntoxicatedOnLife.com/changes to learn more.

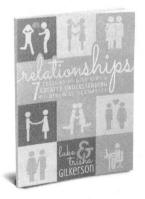

Relationships: 7 Lessons to Give Kids a Greater Understanding of Biblical Sexuality – Designed for parents to use with their children ages 11+, *Relationships* gives parents talking points about how to steward one's own sexuality. Topics include information about gender, lust, masturbation, pornography, modesty, homosexuality, and guarding the heart. Go to IntoxicatedOnLife.com/relationships to learn how you can be notified when it is released in 2016.

Learn more about the whole series at
IntoxicatedOnLife.com/store.

What This Study Is and How to Use It

This is a series of seven devotional Bible studies to read with your child, providing a foundational understanding of godly sexuality. It is sexual education with a biblical core. This series is designed specifically for children ages six to ten, discussed over seven consecutive days.

Why on Earth Did I Write This?

For years, I've worked for a wonderful Christian-owned company called Covenant Eyes. Our software helps protect individuals and families from online pornography.

I love my job because I believe strongly in the mission of our company, but my job also has a dark side. I can confidently say that since shortly after I started working there, not a week has gone by that I have not heard at least one real-life story about how pornography has devastated someone's life.

Each day, I moderate comments on our blog or I talk with others on our team who speak regularly with our members, and the stories are always heart-wrenching. I've spoken with countless wives who felt like their marriages were at the breaking point because of their husbands' obsession with porn. I've received many letters from men who are in prison for possession of child pornography—men who never believed their addictions would have taken them to such perversity. I've spoken with men and women who were exposed to porn when they were eight, nine, ten years old—and now after a decade or two of continued use, they feel like all hope of quitting is lost.

"I wish I would have spoken with my child sooner about sex."

I've also spoken with distraught moms and dads who have just discovered that their child is entrenched in porn before they even had a chance to hear about godly sexuality. In hindsight, most of these parents tell us the same thing: "I wish I would have spoken with my child sooner about sex."

After hearing hundreds of stories, I felt like I was at the tipping point. I wanted to provide a simple, parent-child Bible study that would help start children out on the right foot.

Foundational Building Blocks of Biblical Sexual Values

This series of studies covers basic theological and biological concepts that children in the elementary years can understand. Each study is anchored in a specific text of Scripture.

- Lesson 1 deals with the differences between men and women, giving children a simple understanding of their own bodies and the differences between male and female sexual organs.

- Lesson 2 discusses God's command for the human race to multiply, giving children a basic understanding of sexual intercourse and how babies are conceived.

- Lesson 3 addresses the development of human life in the womb, giving children a picture of the wonder of how babies grow and are born.

- Lesson 4 deals with the intimacy that is created through sex, giving children an understanding of the goodness of sex in marriage and how it creates a strong bond between a man and a woman.

- Lesson 5 discusses the sin of adultery, giving children a biblical understanding of why it is wrong.

- Lesson 6 addresses the difficult subject of rape and sexual abuse, reminding children of the importance of talking to their parents about anyone who touches them in an inappropriate manner. (The average age for first instances of child abuse is just over 9 years old—for both boys and girls; 20% of kids are abused before the age of 8. Most who are abused are hurt by a trusted family member or someone close to the family. For all of these reasons, this is something parents should be sure to discuss with their children.)

- Lesson 7 deals with the importance of honoring God with one's body because God has bought us with a price.

Gross, God, or Good

In some conservative religious or Christian circles, sex is treated as gross, a necessary function they'd rather not talk about.

Our words and tone of voice should communicate to our children that sex is good, something created by God as a blessing.

In the world, sex is treated as a god, an ultimate source of pleasure, meaning, and value.

Neither of these is a right biblical attitude. Sex is not gross. It is not God. But it is good. As parents, it is not only our job to communicate to our children what sex is, but a godly attitude about it. Our words and tone of voice should communicate to our children that sex is good, something created by God as a blessing.

The Fear of Saying "Too Much Too Soon"

For many Christian parents, the biggest question they have when it comes to talking about sex is whether their child is "ready" for it. They fear telling their child too much too soon, awakening sexual interest or curiosity too early, or "saying the wrong thing."

Dr. Margaret Stager from Case Western Reserve wisely says that "too much too soon" is a rare circumstance in today's world. The opposite extreme—your children not knowing your values as they pertain to sex—is far more common and far more dangerous. "Because of the society we live in," she writes, "the consequences of avoiding these conversations far outweigh the consequences of giving too much information too soon."

The fear of too much too soon often means we speak too little too late.

Parent, Are You Ready?

Many times parents' gauge of "readiness" is often not related to anything they see in their child. It is related, rather, to their own sense of sex as a taboo subject—even a shameful subject. They can't picture themselves sitting down across from their sweet little child saying words like "penis" and "vagina" in the same sentence. They can't shake the idea that such topics are "dirty" and not for the ears of innocent children.

Parents must remember, the vast majority of children have not yet learned to think about sex as a taboo subject. Parents are the ones who feel the awkwardness.

This was certainly true for me. Sitting down one evening to give my oldest son a little birds-and-bees conversation, I was most definitely nervous. I had no idea what his reaction would be. But instead of blank stares or awkwardness, I was surprised to see him fully engaged. He asked good questions. He listened attentively. It went on for at least an hour (mostly due to his own curiosity). And at the end of it all he said, "Isn't God amazing?!"

Parents must disregard the myth that merely talking about sex somehow "taints" a young person or makes them want to have sex. Crass humor, sexually provocative images, and our culture's glorification of sex can certainly have a negative impact on a child's mind, but sex itself is not the problem.

The fear of too much too soon often means we speak too little too late.

Parents must face the reality that their children are sexual beings. They may not have reached a stage of raging hormones, but they are curious about matters of gender, intimacy, and the creation of new life. As parents, we should become our children's trusted source of information.

Parents Are Silent While the World is Screaming

For many parents, their aim is to put off sexual conversations as long as possible until the information is absolutely "necessary." They wait until they see the early signs of puberty or until their child is well into puberty. In most instances, this is far too late.

Kids as young as six are coming home from school talking about oral sex, having learned about it on the playground. Sexualized media is everywhere. It is difficult to take a trip to the mall or the grocery store without sexual messages slapping our children across the face. What was once considered indecent is now on the front page of every magazine or brazenly displayed in shopping mall windows. And in a modern world of high speed Internet connections and wi-fi, the question is no longer if your child will see porn someday. The question is when.

With the world screaming sexual messages at children, the last thing they need is their parents' silence about sex.

Why Ages 6 to 10?

Generally speaking, the years between six and ten are a good time to begin conversations about sexual intercourse and God's purposes for sex.

...waiting as long as possible to talk about sex is a risk no parent should be willing to take.

This is only a guideline, of course. Are there exceptional five-year-olds who can have an in-depth conversation about sex? Yes. Are there adolescents who can hear about sex for the first time and still grow up to be sexually godly and healthy adults? Yes. Should every child go through this study at six or seven years old? No. For some children it is wise to wait until they are older. But there are good reasons why introductory conversations about sex work best in this age range.

Foremost, when it comes to parents teaching children about God's purposes for sex, being first is critical. Parents should want to be their child's first and primary source of information about sex. And in a sexually broken world, filled with ungodly messages, waiting as long as possible to talk about sex is a risk no parent should be willing to take.

Second, there are important social, emotional, and intellectual changes that take place in a child's life around the ages of six or seven that can allow our conversations about sexual intercourse to be more fruitful.

From ancient times, cultures have noticed a developmental shift in children around the age of six or seven. The Babylonian Talmud says, "Before the age of six do not accept pupils; from that age you can accept them and stuff them with Torah like an ox." In Medieval times, seven was considered "the age of reason," when children were expected to work alongside adults or begin apprenticeships. In British Common Law, children were not considered responsible for their actions until the age of seven.

Behavioral scientists notice that from six to ten years old, peer relationships become more valuable to children than before. For many children, this is the age when they start attending school, and with school comes the influence of their peers. Because of this, it is important to establish yourself as a source of information about sex before their peers do.

Even homeschooling families are not immune. Children can regularly make contact with other children at church, at friends' homes, and in extra-curricular activities.

Around the age of six (give or take a year), children also tend to form stronger same-sex friendships and they show a strong interest in gender roles. In addition, this is the time when children begin trying to understand how babies are made. It is not uncommon at this stage for children to begin mimicking the intimate behaviors of others (pretending to be married or boyfriend/girlfriend, kissing, holding hands, etc.).

Also around the age of six or seven, a child's intellectual capacities begin to change, allowing you to have more detailed discussions with them about a variety of topics. Before this a child has difficulty understanding things from different points of view. They can only focus on one aspect of an idea at a time. They tend to develop "magical" beliefs because they don't understand cause and effect very well. But around six or seven, a child can begin to distinguish between their own thoughts and the thoughts of others. They can think more logically about objects and events. This makes having discussions with them about detailed subjects much easier.

From the age of seven onward, a child also begins to feel a sense of modesty, desiring privacy when they undress.

 Parents should want to be their child's first and primary source of information about sex.

During these years, a child's body begins gearing up for puberty. An area of the brain called the hypothalamus starts a chain reaction of various hormones in the body, signaling the production of eggs in girls and sperm in boys. On average, this happens between eight and eleven for girls (though it can happen younger) and between nine and eleven for boys. Many of the physical changes will not be visible in these early years, but the internal changes are underway.

Is Your Child Ready for This Study?

Think of the information in this study as seeds you are sowing into your child. In what kinds of soil do these seeds grow best?

The Soil of Familiarity

There is a lot of biological information in these lessons. Ideally, children should grow up in a home very comfortable with conversations about how our bodies work. From early childhood, parents should model a balance of talking frankly about the body and a sense of modesty and propriety. For example, a child should know correct names for body parts and be taught to show respect for privacy. Parents should not be shy or embarrassed about a child's questions but encourage curiosity. Go to IntoxicatedOnLife.com/sex-ed for resources to build a foundation with your younger children (ages three to eight).

The Soil of Formative Teaching

This study assumes you are in a habit of sitting down regularly with your child to read the Bible, pray, and discuss what specific ideas mean. This study assumes you know how to speak to your child in a way that holds his or her attention. These lessons should ideally feel like a normal and natural extension of your family devotions. If this isn't part of the rhythm of your home yet, don't start with this study. Start by establishing a regular routine of conversation about the Bible, coupled with prayer. Get comfortable as a spiritual leader in your home. After you have several months of this under your belt, then consider using this study.

The Soil of Familial Love

Sexual education isn't just taught. It is modeled. Married parents should model what romantic love looks like—honoring and cherishing one another, stealing kisses in the hallway, dancing in the living room, compliments, gifts, etc. Single parents should honor God's standards of celibacy and sexual integrity in their dating relationships. Parents need to model virtues of modesty and honoring the dignity of others—in how we speak about others, in our media choices, and in how we interact. The value and centrality of this modeling cannot be overstated.

Just Give Me a Script

The format of this study is laid out as a script. Feel free to read from these studies verbatim if you find it helpful. If you prefer to read them ahead of time and simply use them as an outline, you can do this as well. Do what feels the most natural.

For a lot of parents, they aren't comfortable having these conversations because no one ever had these conversations with them. They simply don't know what a good parental conversation about sex sounds like. These studies provide you with the words to say.

One of Many Conversations

If there ever was a time when parents could have "the talk" and be done with conversations about sexuality for good, those days are long gone. Teaching children about sex is not a one-time thing. Parents are to teach their children the commands of God repeatedly and in the day-to-day situations of life, "when you sit in your house, and when you walk by the way, and when you lie down, and when you rise" (Deuteronomy 6:7).

These Bible studies provide your child with "foundational" teachings, but after the foundation is laid, more is needed. Repetition is the mother of learning. As time goes on, you'll need to reinforce these lessons in the moment-by-moment situations of life. As your child gets older, you'll want to give more knowledge as it pertains to their growing sexual interests.

In the back of the book you'll find ideas about how to do that.

Swallow Your Fears

When your child has grown up, his or her sexual relationships can bring a deep sense of brokenness and shame or incredible blessing.

Instead of fear, approach this study with a sense of joy and anticipation. Know that this study could be laying a foundation that will set your child up for years of blessing.

When your child has grown up, his or her sexual relationships can bring a deep sense of brokenness and shame or incredible blessing.

the talk

Opening Thought:

Do you remember all the things that God made in the beginning of the world? (*If your child is familiar with the book of Genesis, see what he or she can remember about the creation of light, waters, sky, land, sun, moon, stars, sea creatures, flying creatures, land animals, and lastly human beings.*)

I want to read to you the story of the last day of creation so that you know how God made human beings different from everything else in creation.

Scripture Reading: Genesis 1:24-27

Explanation: God made all kinds of creatures to live on the land, including human beings.

Humans were created different from every other creature. Genesis says we are created "in the image of God." This means that, unlike all the animals, we were created to be like God: compassionate to others, gracious, patient, loving, truthful, forgiving, and just. We were created by God to take care of this world and its creatures.

But God didn't just create one kind of human being. He created two. The Bible says God made us male and female. He created both men and women. Men and women are similar in a lot of ways. How are boys and girls similar? Can you think of anything that makes us alike? (*See what your child can come up with. You might point out obvious physical similarities: two eyes, a nose, a mouth. You might point out other similarities like the ability to talk, walk on two legs, think about complex things, the ability to build and invent complex tools, etc.*) Both men and women are created in the image of God, which means both men and women deserve the same respect—both boys and girls are of great value to God. But there are some very important differences between men and women.

God made men and women with different body parts, both inside and out. Let me show you what I mean.

Talking Points:

Show your child the Male Anatomy and Female Anatomy *diagrams. If necessary, use the talking points provided below.*

Access free videos of the growth process at <u>IntoxicatedOnLife.com/sex-ed</u>.

FEMALE ANATOMY

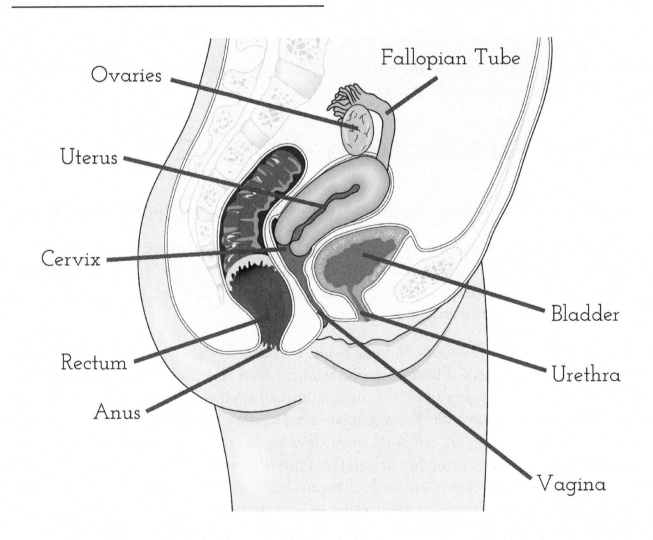

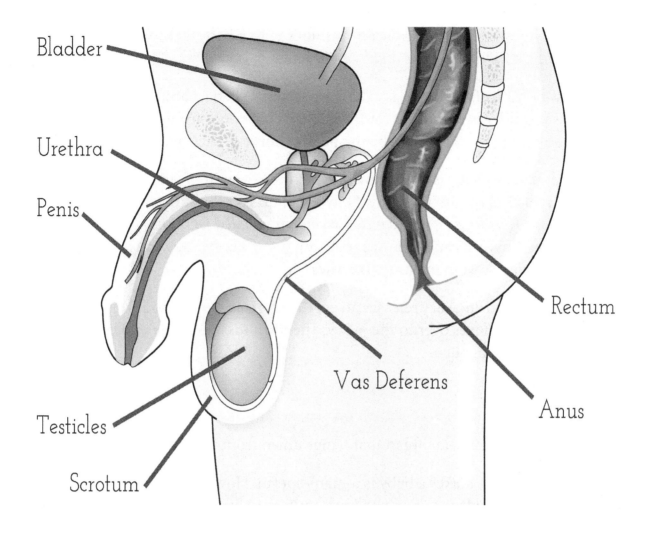

Bladder

Urethra

Penis

Testicles

Scrotum

Vas Deferens

Rectum

Anus

Male and Female Similarities

- A woman's body and a man's body are similar in certain ways. Both men and women have a bladder for holding urine. Both men and women have a rectum for holding solid waste.

- For both men and women, their urine comes through the urethra and the solid waste comes out through the anus.

Female Anatomy

- God made women with another opening that men do not have. This is called the vagina. So, men have two openings and women have three.

- If you go farther up into a woman's body from the vagina you come to the uterus. A woman's body is designed by God to hold and grow a baby. The uterus is the special place where a baby grows. Do you know any families with a baby right now? (*See if your child can name any families that have a baby right now.*)

- The narrow bottom of the uterus is called the cervix. When a baby is ready to be born, this area opens up wider to make way for the baby to come out through the vagina. It is amazing how God designed women to be the perfect home for a growing baby.

- Part of what makes a baby is a woman's egg, but these eggs aren't the size of eggs you might eat for breakfast. These are very tiny. How small do you think they are? (*Have your child hold up their fingers to see if they can show you how small a woman's egg might be.*) Actually, an egg is so tiny you can't even see one with just your eye. A woman's eggs are formed inside the ovaries. A woman has two ovaries.

- About once a month an ovary releases an egg. This is called ovulation. When this happens, the fallopian tube moves over to the ovary. Then thin tissues at the end of the tube gently sweep the egg into the tube.

Male Anatomy

- Men have a penis. This is an organ that hangs down from the front of a man's body.

- Another part of what makes a baby is a man's sperm. How small do you think sperm are? (*Again, have your child guess how small these cells are.*) Just like an egg, sperm are too small to see with just your eyes. Actually, one sperm is even smaller than an egg. Sperm are created in the testicles. Men have two testicles just like women have two ovaries.

- Testicles are inside a layer of skin and muscle called the scrotum. This hangs down underneath the penis.

- Sperm travel through the vas deferens. This name means "a duct that carries away." That's what the vas deferens does: carries sperm away into the urethra in the penis.

- When a sperm from the man unites with an egg from the woman, a baby is made. Later on we'll talk about how they come together.

- To summarize, both men and women have a lot of similarities. We are both made in the image of God, and we are both very special to God, but men and women have different parts inside and out. Can you remember what some of these parts are? (*See if your child can name any of the parts you discussed. Show him or her the diagrams again and see if they can remember what the different parts do.*)

Questions for Your Child:

1. What is the one new thing you learned about your own body? What is one new thing you learned about the body of the opposite sex? *(Depending on the gender of your child, find out what parts of his or her own anatomy they found really interesting. Get your child talking about what he or she found intriguing about the opposite sex.)*

2. What does it mean to be created in the image of God? *(It means we are like God in ways that nothing else is like God. We are the creatures God made to care for this world that He has made.)*

Important Disclaimer for Your Child:

This is all very interesting information, but it is important that parents share this with their children. You shouldn't talk about any of this with your friends, because that's their parents' job, not yours. Don't bring this up around them, and if anyone brings it up to you, just tell them that it isn't an appropriate conversation.

Prayer: Oh God, You have made us a little lower than the angels, but You crowned us with glory and honor, made in your image (Psalm 8:5-6). Help us to honor everyone we see, boys and girls, knowing they are made in Your image. Thank you also for making us different. Amen.

Opening Thought:

D o you remember what we talked about last time? What do you remember about the differences between male and female? (*See how much your child remembers about male anatomy and female anatomy. Pull out the diagrams again and review.*)

Today I want to talk about one of the reasons God created us male and female.

Scripture Reading: Genesis 1:28-31

Explanation: Remember what we talked about last time: Human beings are created in God's image. We are the ones God put in charge to care for His world. But the first man and woman were only two people, and the world is a very big place. How were just two people going to take care of the whole world? (*See if your child comes up with any ideas. Did God expect Adam and Eve to take care of the whole world by themselves?*)

The very first command God gave to the first man and woman was to multiply and fill the earth. They were supposed to have babies who would grow up and have babies of their own who would grow up and have more babies. God wants human beings to have children so we can spread throughout the whole world. Right now there are billions of people on the earth, and every person is related to the first man and woman who existed.

I want to explain to you how men and women have babies.

Talking Points:

Show your child the Male Anatomy *and* Female Anatomy *diagrams. If necessary, use the talking points provided below.*

Access free videos of the growth process at IntoxicatedOnLife.com/sex-ed.

FEMALE ANATOMY

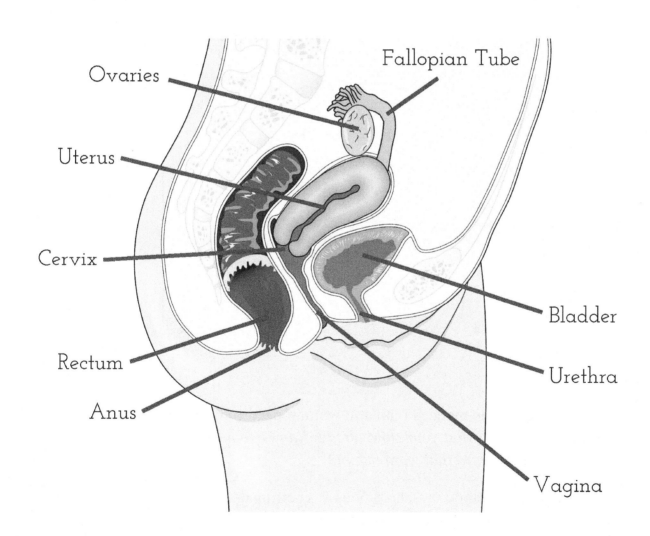

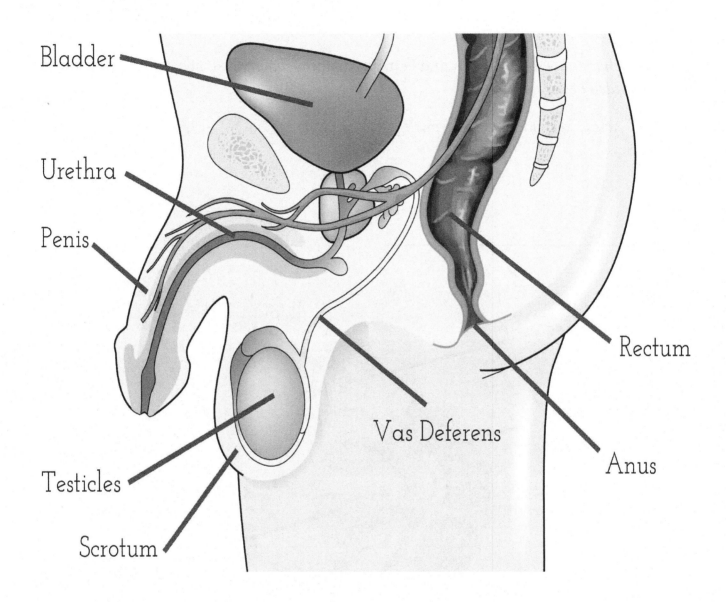

Bladder

Urethra

Penis

Testicles

Scrotum

Vas Deferens

Rectum

Anus

- In order for babies to be made, a man and woman need to have sex. Have you ever heard that word before? (*See what your child already knows about the word "sex" and see where he or she might have heard that word before.*)

- A man's penis is full of blood vessels. When he is getting ready to have sex, these blood vessels will fill with blood making his penis very hard and straight. This is called an erection.

- This allows him to insert his penis inside the woman's vagina. This is called having sex. It is the way God designed us to not only have babies but also to feel close to the person we are married to. It makes husband and wife feel a special bond with each other.

- Then the man's penis does something called ejaculation. This means a fluid called semen comes out of the penis.

- This semen contains lots of sperm. Do you remember what sperm is? (*See if your child can remember.*) How many sperm do you think a man can release at one time when he ejaculates? (*See if your child can guess the number.*) A man can release around 40 million sperm at one time, and sometimes he can release a whole lot more, sometimes over a billion. Those sperm start swimming through the woman's body to get to the egg.

- Sometimes, a man and woman have sex and the woman's body hasn't released an egg at that time. This means the sperm will just swim for a few days and eventually die.

- But if a woman has released an egg, this means she could get pregnant.

- The sperm swim up through the cervix, into the uterus, and then up through the fallopian tubes.

- Close to the ovary, at the opening of the fallopian tube, an egg might be there for a sperm to fertilize.

- A lot of sperm die along the way. Only a small fraction of them make it to the uterus. Of those, only a small fraction make it to the fallopian tubes. Of those, only a small fraction make it to the egg. God made it so that only the sperm that are strong enough and healthy enough are the ones that get to the egg.

- Only one sperm fertilizes the egg. After one sperm gets inside the egg, no other sperm can come inside.

- The sperm and the egg combine their material to make a single living cell. That small cell is so small you can't even see it with just your eyes, but it is the beginning of a human being. So, did you start out that small? *(Yes.)* Did I start out that small? *(Yes.)*

- So, to summarize: Married men and women have sex as a way to show love to each other. He releases sperm from his penis into her body. One of those sperm might fertilize an egg, creating a new life! Isn't it amazing how God made our bodies?

Questions for Your Child:

1. Do you remember: what is the name of the swimming cells that are inside a man's testicles? *(Sperm)*

2. What is the name of the special cells that are inside the woman's ovaries? *(Eggs)*

3. What happens when they come together? *(A new human being is made)*

4. How does the sperm get inside the woman's body to fertilize the egg? *(A man and a woman have sex. This means the man inserts his penis into the woman's vagina, and he releases his sperm inside her body.)*

5. Why does God want human beings to have babies? *(So we can multiply in number and spread throughout the earth.)*

Prayer: God, thank You for the way a man and a woman come together to make another human being. You fashioned every person—rich and poor, master and servant—in the womb of their mother (Job 31:15). Children are a gift from You (Psalm 127:3). Help us to remember that when we talk to others, knowing You created them in Your image. Amen.

LESSON 3: WONDERFULLY MADE

Opening Thought:

Do you remember what we talked about last time? How are babies made? (*See how much your child remembers. You might want to pull out the anatomy diagrams to refresh your child's memory and review some of the major talking points.*)

When a baby first comes into existence, you can't even see it with your eyes because it is so small. But over time that baby grows and grows. That's what we'll talk about today.

Scripture Reading: Psalm 139:13-18

Explanation: In this psalm, the author is praising God for the day when he was conceived in his mother's womb. Even when he was too tiny for anyone else to see, God could see him.

Even when he was only a small bundle of cells, God didn't just see a blob; He saw a person.

Even when it was the first day of his life in his mother's womb, God could see into the future and see every day of his life to come.

When the author thought about the way God paid him special attention and put him together inside his mother's womb, he was amazed.

Today we actually know what a baby looks like as it is growing inside the womb. The more we know about this, the more we can be amazed at how God knit us together before we were born.

Talking Points:

Show your child the How a Baby Grows *diagrams. If necessary, use the talking points provided.*

Access free videos of the growth process at <u>IntoxicatedOnLife.com/sex-ed</u>.

HOW A BABY GROWS

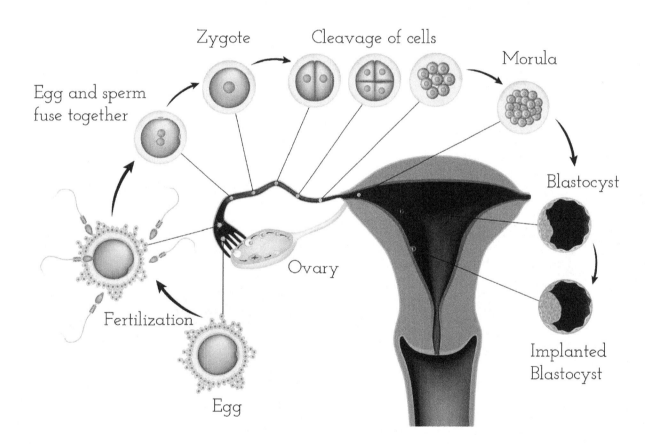

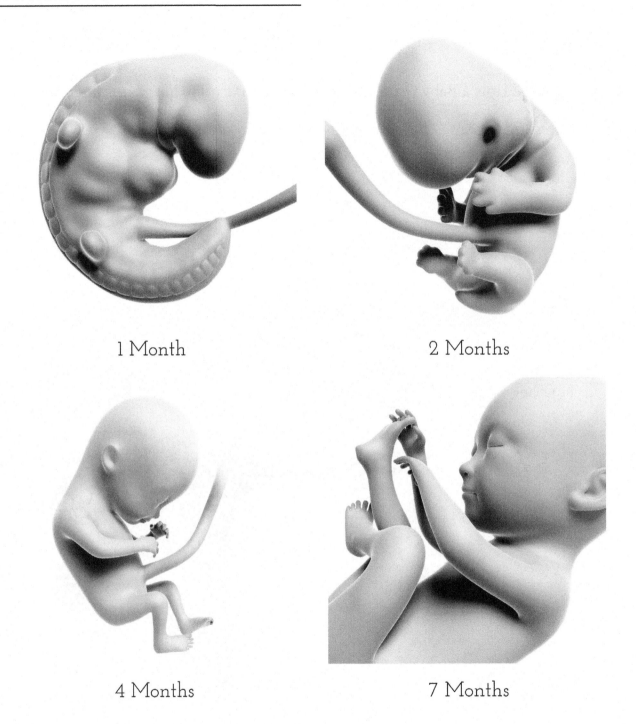

1 Month

2 Months

4 Months

7 Months

- Let's say a man and woman have sex shortly after her ovary has released an egg. The egg is at the far end of the fallopian tube.

- When one of the sperm finally breaks through the protective layer of the egg, it enters the egg. This is called fertilization.

- Then the material from the sperm combines with the material from the egg, coming together to make a human being.

- This forms a single cell called a zygote. The zygote is only one cell, but it contains all the information inside it to produce a full-grown human being.

- Then the cell begins to do something called cleavage, which means the first cell divides into two cells. Then those two cells divide into four cells. Then those four cells divide into eight cells.

- Once the baby has divided into 16 cells, it starts to look a little like a mulberry. The Latin word for mulberry is "morus" which is why the baby is called a morula. It only takes a few days for a zygote to become a morula.

- After about five days, the baby is known as a blastocyst. It has an inner group of cells and an outer group. The inner group becomes the baby's body (*or embryo*). The outer group of cells becomes what's known as the placenta. The placenta is the thing that gives the baby its nutrients while it is growing.

- Finally the baby is implanted in the uterus. This is where it will grow for up to nine months.

- At about one month the baby is the size of a poppy seed. How big is a poppy seed? (Have your child guess how big. Hold up your fingers to show 2mm or if you have a poppy seed, show one to your child.) Even though it is that small, it already has a tube that will later form into the baby's spine and brain.

- The baby is fed through something called the umbilical cord. It goes into the baby's digestive system and is connected to the placenta.

- After about two months the baby is the size of a cranberry. How big is a cranberry? (*Have your child hold up his or her fingers to show you and correct them if need be.*) Even at that size, it already has the beginnings of a brain, heart, blood, arms, legs, eyes, ears, nose, cheeks, and chin.

- By the end of four months, the baby has developed bones, fingernails, fingerprints, vocal chords, and the ability to hear. It might even be sucking its thumb. At this stage it is about the size of an onion.

- By the end of seven months, the baby is as long as a cucumber and is swallowing, hiccuping, yawning, sleeping, kicking, and punching.

- The baby is considered full grown at nine months.

Questions for Your Child:

1. Do you remember the part of the mom's body in which a baby is implanted? *(Uterus)*

2. What is the full amount of time a baby can live inside its mother? *(Nine months)*

3. How does a baby get all its food while it is growing? *(The placenta and the umbilical cord)*

4. How does the baby come out of its mother? *(Through the woman's vagina)*

Prayer: God, there is so much we don't know about how a body is formed in a mother's womb (Ecclesiastes 11:5). You are the One who puts us together. You are the One who had thousands of thoughts about us before anyone knew we existed. You fashion the hearts of all people (Psalm 33:15). Help us to remember that we are works of art. Amen.

the talk

Opening Thought:

Last time we talked about how babies grow inside their mothers, but do you remember how babies start? How are babies conceived? (*A sperm from a man fertilizes an egg inside a woman.*)

We talked before about sex. This is when a man and a woman are naked together and the man inserts his penis into the woman's vagina. Men and women do this not just so they can have a baby. The Bible has a lot more to say about sex.

Scripture Reading: Genesis 2:18-25

Explanation: God made the first man, Adam, and then He said it wasn't right that Adam should be all alone. He wanted to put Adam into a family, and then He wanted Adam's family to grow and grow to fill the world. The first step was to create a woman to be his wife.

God caused Adam to fall asleep, and He took some bone and some flesh from Adam's side and closed up the wound in Adam's skin. From that bone and flesh he built the most beautiful of all His creatures: a woman.

When Adam woke up and saw her, he burst out with a poem of excitement. He knew right away she was the one who would be his companion. She had come from his own body, so he knew she was his perfect match.

Why would God take part of Adam's side to make Eve? (*See what your child says.*) He could have made Eve however He wanted, but He was teaching Adam something. What do you think God was teaching Adam when He made Eve this way? (*See what your child says.*) He wanted them to have a close, loving relationship, to remember that they belonged together.

He wanted them to be connected in a special way. Adam and Eve were the very first married couple.

This is what getting married and having sex are all about. Today, when a man and a woman have sex, the Bible says they become "one flesh." This means they are united in a special way—in their bodies, their minds, and their hearts. God made sex very pleasurable and exciting. Sex is not just about making a baby—many times people have sex and they don't conceive babies. Sex is something that makes you feel connected to someone.

Sex is so powerful, it creates a special bond between a man and a woman. This is why you should only have sex with someone you are married to. God says that if you are going to enjoy sex with someone, you need to be committed to stay with them as long as you both are alive. This is what marriage is all about.

For the same reason, even if a person isn't married yet, they shouldn't have sex. Sex was designed by God to be a special bond between a husband and a wife. Of course, God can forgive people when they sin, but God wants us to only have sex when we are married for our own good. We don't want to form a special bond with someone like that only to have them leave us. God doesn't want us to get close to someone like that until we've decided to spend the rest of our lives with that person.

Questions for Your Child:

1. Do you think you'll be married some day? *(See what your child says. Whether they say they think they'll be married or single, affirm either one as a good desire.)*

2. If someone had sex with someone else who wasn't their spouse and then that person left forever, how do you think they would feel? *(You would feel very lonely and sad. Sex makes you feel connected to someone, and if they aren't committed to staying with you for life, you would feel very sad when they were gone.)*

3. What words does the Bible use to describe this special bond between two people? *(One flesh)*

4. Should someone have sex with a person they aren't married to? *(No. It is against God's law, and it is harmful to those who do it.)*

Prayer: God, thank You for creating marriage. I pray that, if [child's name] will be married someday, You guard and protect their marriage so they will stay married as long as they both live (Matthew 19:6). Give [child's name] wisdom in choosing if and when to get married, and give him/her joy in marriage. Amen.

LESSON 5: YOU SHALL NOT COMMIT ADULTERY

Opening Thought:

Has someone ever stolen something from you? How do you think it feels if someone takes something of yours? (*Have your child imagine what that would feel like.*) But what if someone stole the person you were married to? How would that feel? (*It would be even more painful.*)

Today we're going to talk more about sex and a sin called "adultery."

Scripture Reading: Exodus 20:1-2, 12-17

Explanation: In this passage, God is giving His people Ten Commandments. These are ten special laws Israel is meant to live by. He tells them about how they should relate to other people. Children should honor and obey their parents. People should never murder one another. They should never steal from one another. They should never lie about another person. They should never desire to take anything that belongs to another person. God also talks about sex in these commandments.

Men and women were designed by God to be attracted to each other, and many people grow up and get married to someone. Someday, if God chooses, you may find someone you want to serve and love for the rest of your life, someone to be your spouse.

But what would happen if one day your spouse decided they wanted to act like they were married to someone else too? What if they started going out on dates with someone else? Spending a lot of time with that person? Hugging and kissing that person? Even having sex with that person? This would be very sad, because marriage is supposed to be between one man and one woman. When married people have sex with someone who isn't their spouse, or when a person has sex with someone who is married to somebody else, this is called adultery.

Not only should we stay away from adultery, but we should also remove from our hearts any desire to do it.

Having sex with someone who is married to someone else isn't just sinful because it is misusing sex. It is also sinful because it is stealing from someone else.

Questions for Your Child:

1. Many people in the world don't follow God's commandments, but what would happen if everyone in the world stopped trying to follow them? What would the world be like? *(It would be a terrible place to live. It would be a place of theft, murder, and chaos.)*

2. What is adultery? *(Adultery is sex between a married person and someone else who is not that person's spouse.)*

3. Why do you think people commit adultery? *(They commit adultery because they get attracted to someone who isn't their spouse, so they want to get close to them. They end up caring more about what they want and less about what is right.)*

Prayer: Oh God, thank You for creating marriage. We know the person who commits adultery lacks sense (Proverbs 6:32). Give [child's name] wisdom to know how to guard his/her heart. Help us all to honor marriage the way you do (Hebrews 13:4). Amen.

LESSON 6: DO NOT VIOLATE ME

Opening Thought:

Do you remember what the Bible calls the special bond two people have when they have sex? (*One flesh*)

What is it called when someone who is married has sex with someone else? (*Adultery*)

Like I've said before, sex is very powerful. It makes you feel close to someone. Sometimes people desire to have sex so much, it makes them do really hurtful things. That's what this next story is about.

Scripture Reading: 2 Samuel 13:1-2, 6-14

Explanation: Ammon is one of King David's sons, and he falls in love with his relative Tamar.

He thinks she is beautiful and wants to have sex with her. He's overwhelmed by this desire.

So he thinks up a plan so he can get near her. He pretends to be sick and asks his father to send in Tamar to take care of him. When they are alone together, he tells her he wants to have sex with her. She's shocked and tells him, "Do not violate me. This sin should never be committed in Israel, among God's people." But he doesn't care. He wants to be with her so badly, he rapes her. Rape is when someone forces someone else to have sex when they don't want to.

Can you imagine how Tamar felt? Tricked by her own relative? Forced to have sex? It would have been awful. Sadly, all over the world, hundreds of thousands of women and even men are sexually abused every year.

I'm telling this to you because it is important that if anyone tries to make you have sex, or if anyone touches your private areas without your permission, you should tell me as soon as you can. You should tell me no matter who tries to do this to you—even if it is someone you love, like a family member. It isn't right if someone touches you in a sexual way or they try to get you to have sex. You should always tell them "No," that you don't like to be touched that way. If something like that happens, it is important to tell me right away so we can stop it from happening again. Even if the person threatens to hurt you or hurt someone you love if you tell, you should still tell me. This is not a good secret to keep.

Questions for Your Child:

1. How do you think Tamar felt after this thing happened with Ammon? *(She was devastated. The story goes on to say that she was so ashamed she never got married to anyone.)*

2. Has anyone ever tried to touch you in a sexual way? *(Listen carefully to what your child has to say.)*

Prayer: Oh God, You hate when people misuse sex, especially when they force other people to do it. Right now, we know there are thousands of people out there who are experiencing this terrible crime. We ask that You give justice to the weak and afflicted (Psalm 82:3). Help the church to seek justice and encourage those who are abused by others (Isaiah 1:17). Amen.

LESSON 7: BOUGHT WITH A PRICE

Opening Thought:

Can you think of something that people pay lots of money for? (*See what ideas your child comes up with. Cars. Houses. Boats.*)

What if you paid a lot of money for something, like a car, and gave it to someone as a gift. Then that person started driving it recklessly, crashing it into walls? How would you feel? (*You would probably feel offended that they were misusing the very expensive gift you gave them.*)

Today I want to talk to you about something God purchased for a very high price: your body.

Scripture Reading: 1 Corinthians 6:18-20

Explanation: Our bodies are a wonderful gift from God. God gave us many pleasures that have to do with our bodies. He gave us tongues to enjoy the taste of food. He gave us noses to enjoy different smells. He gave us eyes so we can look at beautiful things. We can also use our bodies to be close to the people we love, to touch, to hug, to kiss.

Sex is also something enjoyable for married couples to do. It makes them feel close to one another. Unlike anything else, sex brings two people together in a special way, making them feel connected.

This is why sexual sin is different from any other sin. If we have sex with someone it makes us feel a strong bond with them, but if they aren't married to us and then they leave us, it's like our bodies feel that something is missing.

We should never think our bodies are just for fun or pleasurable experiences. Our bodies belong to God. If you are a Christian, God's Holy Spirit lives inside you. Your body is a temple of the Spirit. Just like in the Old Testament when God showed His presence in the temple made of stone and wood, right now He lives inside His people.

As Christians, our bodies belong to God because God bought us. The price He paid was the death of His Son, the highest price He could pay. When Jesus died on the cross, he didn't just pay the price for our sins so our souls could go to heaven after we die. He paid for our bodies as well. Some day, when Jesus returns, our bodies will be raised from the grave and transformed to be just like His glorious body.

There's only one person who can tell us how to use our bodies: God Himself. He has told us how to treat our bodies in His Word. He is the One who bought us with a price.

Questions for Your Kids:

1. What do you think about the idea of having a glorious body like Jesus' resurrection body? *(See what your kids think about this. Remind them of stories of what the disciples saw when Jesus rose from the dead, how His body was different. If time permits, read from 1 Corinthians 15:3-8 and 42-44.)*

2. If God is the One who owns our bodies, how should we treat them? *(We should take care of them.)*

3. Why is it important to follow God's rules about sex? *(First, because God is the one who made our bodies. Second, He is the one who bought us for Himself through the death of Christ. Third, because sexual sin harms us in a way no other sin does. It connects us to another person. If we aren't married to that person, and they go away, it will make us feel very lonely.)*

Prayer: Oh God, You bought us with a price. You paid for our sins in full on the cross. Help us to treat our bodies with respect because we know our bodies do not belong to us. We believe someday our bodies will be immortal, glorious, and powerful (1 Corinthians 15:42-43). As we grow, help us to use our eyes, hands, and minds in a pure way. Amen.

WHAT'S NEXT?

These studies are only the beginning. Now that your child has a foundational understanding of sex and sexuality from God's point of view, it is important to remind him or her of these lessons and to build on them.

Let the Bible Break the Ice for You

Reminding your child about these lessons from time to time will help to firm up these concepts in his or her mind. One of the best ways to do this is to simply read the Bible without trying to "sanitize" it. There are many, many stories in the Bible that address the subjects of sex, marriage, and intimacy. Simply be true to the stories when you read them.

For example, when Abraham and Hagar conceive Ishmael (Genesis 16), you can ask your child if they remember what sexual intercourse is and why adultery is wrong.

When Jacob and Esau are conceived (Genesis 25), you can remind your child about how sperm and egg come together to conceive a child (and even teach them about how more than one egg can be fertilized at a time, bringing about fraternal twins).

When Joseph flees from Potiphar's wife (Genesis 39), you can reinforce the importance of fleeing from sexual temptations.

When you read about Solomon's 700 wives and 300 concubines (1 Kings 11), you can remind your child about the importance of not allowing love or sex to pull your heart away from following God.

Virtually every book of the Bible contains allusions or references to sexual topics. As the Bible brings sex into the story, bring sex into your conversations.

Finding Teachable Moments

Reminding your child about your sexual values can also happen in the day-to-day moments of life.

- Your child is always learning about his or her body. Use these discoveries as opportunities to talk.

- If something is shown on TV, in either entertainment or news, that touches on sexual topics, be sure to add your own commentary. If sexual immorality is portrayed in a positive light, be sure ask your child, "What's wrong about the way they are presenting this?"

- Weddings and pregnancies are also great opportunities to remind your child about the goodness of sex and marriage. When you see a pregnant woman, you might ask, "Do you remember how babies are conceived?" or "How big do you think that woman's baby is right now?"

- Don't be frightened if your child receives misinformation about sex from one of their friends. If your child says something like, "I heard you can't get pregnant the first time you have sex," simply respond by correcting them. This is another great teachable moment.

- Animal behavior also provides another opportunity to remind children about sexuality. If your child is learning about mating habits of animals in school, or if your child sees animals mating at the zoo, or if you have pets that are "caught in the act," use these opportunities to remind your child about what he or she has learned.

Internet Accountability is Critical

Most Christian parents know about Internet filtering. This is a great place to start to protect your children from pornography and other sexual media online.

As children get older, it is important to not just protect them from harmful and tempting images online; we must also prepare them to guard their own eyes. There is no better way to do this than to use Internet Accountability software. Monitor everywhere your kids go online and have regular conversations at home about how to best use the Internet. This helps them to think twice about where they go online, training them to be their own watchdogs.

Covenant Eyes has Accountability and Filtering for computers, phones, and tablets. Learn more in the back of this book and use the promo code THETALK when you sign up for the service to get your first month of service free.

Beyond the Middle Childhood Years

For the ages of ten to twelve, other lessons about sexuality are very important. These lessons should include, but not be limited to, changes their body and mind will undergo, talking about masturbation (especially its connection to lust and orgasm), nocturnal emissions, oral sex, and STDs. Biblical lessons should probably include lessons about how to guard their hearts

(Proverbs 4:23) and eyes (Job 31:1), how to avoid temptation (Proverbs 7), and the beauty and power of falling in love (Song of Solomon 3:5).

Into puberty, parents should help their teens understand and navigate the changes they are experiencing. At this point, nothing is really "off limits" in terms of conversation topics.

Parents should continue to be sources of godly information about sex, including the fact that God created sexual arousal as a good thing (Proverbs 5:19; Song of Solomon 1:2) but lust is a sin that must be radically opposed (Matthew 5:27-28). Parents should give guidelines and boundaries about dating and courtship, oral sex and other forms of "making out," as well as pornography and media choices.

A Promise to Remember

The book of Proverbs, written especially for the young, warns its readers many times about the seduction of lust and easy sex. But the readers are promised they can avoid the snare of sexual sin. How?

> …keep your father's commandment,
> and forsake not your mother's teaching.
> Bind them on your heart always;
> tie them around your neck.
> When you walk, they will lead you;
> when you lie down, they will watch over you;
> and when you awake, they will talk with you. (Proverbs 6:20-22)

Be encouraged. Your words have power. Your commands are life-giving. Your teachings are critical. In years to come, the echoes of your voice will watch over your children even in the darkest corners of temptation.

Adultery — Sex between a married person and someone else who is not that person's spouse

Anus — The opening between a person's buttocks where solid waste comes out

Bladder — The organ in the body that holds urine before it leaves the body

Blastocyst — An embryo with a single layer of cells surrounding a round cavity of fluid

Cervix — The narrow end at the opening of a woman's uterus

Cleavage — The act of cells splitting apart to form new cells

Egg — A cell that is produced in the ovaries that can combine with sperm to make a baby

Ejaculation — The release of semen from the penis

Embryo — An early stage of a baby's life while in the womb

Erection — The state in which a man's penis becomes firm and elongated

Fallopian tubes — A pair of tubes that carry eggs from the ovaries to the uterus

Fertilization — The process of a sperm uniting with an egg to form a zygote

Image of God — A term used in the Bible to describe the special relationship human beings have with God and their special likeness with God.

Morula — A mass of cells formed by cleavage of a zygote before becoming a blastocyst

One flesh — A term the Bible uses to describe the special bond between people created by having sex

Ovaries — A pair of organs in a woman that produce eggs and female hormones

Ovulation — The release of a mature egg from an ovary

Penis — The organ on the front of a man's body used for sex and releasing urine

Placenta — An organ that forms with a baby to supply the unborn baby with nutrients

Rectum — The last part of the large intestine that helps digest food and stores solid waste

Scrotum — The sac of skin that contains a man's testicles

Semen — A sticky, whitish liquid that contains sperm that is ejaculated through the penis

Sperm — A cell that is produced in the testicles that can combine with an egg to make a baby

Testicles — A pair of organs in a man that produce sperm and male hormones

Umbilical cord — A long, narrow tube that connects an unborn baby to the placenta

Urethra — The tube through which urine moves from the bladder out of the body

Uterus — A muscular organ in a woman's body in which a baby grows before birth

Vagina — The passage leading from the uterus to outside the body

Vas deferens — A duct that carries sperm from the testicles to the penis

Zygote — A fertilized egg; a single cell formed by the combination of egg and sperm

Made in the USA
Coppell, TX
06 April 2022